THE STORY OF
HENNELIE HAMSTER
RUNNING
WILD AT CHRISTMAS TIME
ON A FARM
IN ZIMBABWE

BY NIKKI ZIEHL

Copyright © 2012 Nikki Ziehl
All rights reserved.
ISBN: 1478240954
ISBN 13: 9781478240952

RUNNING WILD tells the story of Hennelie Hamster who, miraculously at Christmas time, escapes from her cage in a farm house in Africa and flees from the humans and her so called partner, vindictive, cruel Harry Hamster, into the wilderness in search of freedom.

On her journey she encounters many strange domestic and wild creatures, some threatening, others friendly.

During her ambitious mission she discovers that she is on a tobacco farm in Zimbabwe.

Will Hennelie's faith in her Creator help her survive in the bushveld?

Does she ever find the love, peace, happiness and contentment that she yearns for?

Will the forces of darkness succeed in keeping Hennelie from her destiny?

This book is dedicated to the Creator of
"All things Bright and Beautiful,
All Creatures Great and Small"
Thank you for all your Blessings.

Mikki Ziehl

ACKNOWLEDGEMENTS

My son Kent, you make me so proud. You are a true blessing and I'm so grateful for you. You have given me such purpose in life. My mum Rosemary, you have been such an inspiration to me. You are so talented and make such a lovely warm home. You do so much for everyone; a real giver. My dad Ken, you have been the best father ever, you bring such fun and laughter into the home, you have always provided so well for your family. Your wisdom and advice is so appreciated. Thank you for always encouraging us to keep trying with one of your favourite sayings *nothing ventured nothing gained*. Growing up on *Recondite Farm* was beautiful. My sister Julie, you love all creatures so much. I've lost count of all the animals you've rescued in your lifetime. You are so kind and so generous. You make me laugh so much with your stories. My sister Debbie, you are an angel; thank you for always lending an ear. Thank you for your patience; for always listening and offering guidance and for believing in me always. Thank you for all your prayers. My brother Kenyon, who is so philosophical and gentle, you are such a good person with a heart of gold. I love you all.

Now for the relatives dotted all over the world. What an amazing bunch you are. I am so proud to be a part of this unusual, spirited, generous and kind clan of characters. It's always open house with these special people; where everyone is made to feel welcome in their homes; where there's always enough to go around. I am so grateful for you.

To my friends, who have always been behind me and supported me, thank you. Especially Jackie Whyte, my son's godmother; what an extraordinary person you are. Thank you so much for your help always in every which way; your deeds will never be forgotten. Thank you for all the good laughs.

To all Zimbabweans, you are unique and special; each of you deserves the very best that life has to offer.

CONTENTS

The Great Escape

11

Crossroads

33

The Bushveld

53

THE GREAT ESCAPE

"Please, please, please," whined the little girl as she picked her nose and casually wiped her snotty fingers on the car seat.

"Please Gran," begged the boy with his dimpled cheeks stuffed with jelly babies. "We'll look after them properly and play with them a lot, please Gran."

The children's indulgent granny gave in and purchased the two hamsters from the pet shop in Harare. They were handpicked carefully by the grubby children and shoved unceremoniously together into a small, cold, white cage.

"This one is mine," said the boy greedily. "He's a boy and I'm a boy, I'm going to call him Harry, Harry Hamster." He smirked pleased with himself.

"This one's a girl, she's mine," said the girl snatching at fur. "I'm going to call her Hennelie, after Hennelie Van Aard, the lady in the ice-cream parlour. Look! She looks just like her, small and round with yellow hair. Hennelie, Hennelie."

"Van Arse," sniggered the boy.

"I hope they have babies," cooed the girl.

"Oh that'll be cool," cried the boy excitedly. "Then we can sell them."

What a long and horrible week it had been for poor Hennelie. Not only was she at the mercy of the children's podgy fingers and rough handling, she was also at the mercy of Harry

Hamster, her own kind, who as it turned out was an A-class, first prize, fat, pompous, cruel, bully.

"If I don't get away from Harry soon, I know I will die," twitched Hennelie anxiously.

It wasn't uncommon for hamsters to kill each other. In the pet shop the creatures often discussed the terrible murders that occurred between hamsters.

The female hamsters were forever being warned to protect their young from the male hamsters who enjoyed guzzling them for fun.

"It's horrific, horrific." Hennelie recalled the parakeets screeching in the pet shop. It made her feel so ashamed for her hamster race.

Hennelie felt very frightened, especially since she secretly suspected that she was expecting babies of her own in the not too distant future.

And yes, Harry was the father. This made her feel even more queasy and uneasy and even more determined to make, as the pet shop owner would say, "chop chop" escape plans in order to protect herself and her new family.

"Fear," thought Hennelie, "must be the very worst emotion of all, I must not let it grip me, for then I become quite helpless and cannot think clearly."

She stood on her back legs; her tiny pink paws rubbed at her pink nose quickly, nervously. Twitching her whiskers her little black eyes surveyed her surroundings.

At the back of the cage near the container which held the seeds, Hennelie spotted a couple of bars that looked slightly wider than the rest. She scurried nearer to them for a closer examination. Nibbling energetically on a sunflower seed between her dainty paws she studied the size of the gap. "Surely I'll be able to squeeze through those bars," she contemplated, chewing furiously.

Mentally she marked this area as point A in her escape route plan. Hennelie grabbed a thick rough shell which contained a peanut, and gave it a hard bite with her two sharp front teeth. Holding it firmly she attacked it with frenzied gnawing whilst she very carefully scrutinized the surroundings beyond the bars.

"What a horrid room to be deposited into," thought Hennelie with a shudder, "what sickly pale green walls, no windows, no fresh air, nothing but the tatty remains of crushed cobwebs. I feel nauseous. I must get out of here."

Despair took a hold of Hennelie. She released her grip on the peanut shell which plopped pathetically onto the damp sawdust. Rubbing her eyes she chanted to herself, "I mustn't lose hope, I mustn't lose hope."

Like so many other lonely and desperate creatures Hennelie had taken to talking to herself softly, silently, but now there was a sense of urgency in her voice, she groaned louder than usual, "*I must not lose hope!* There must be a way out of this room, come on Hennelie find a way. Look again." She stood upright bowed her head and whispered, "Please help me find my path to freedom."

The humans had put a small yellow ladder into the cage for the hamsters to climb. Harry hogged the upper cubicle, whilst Hennelie preferred to stay downstairs, well away from him.

Fortunately, Harry was dozing, which gave Hennelie the opportunity of scurrying halfway up the ladder to take a better look at the claustrophobic room again to look for a way out. Her tiny eyes scanned the room a second time. She saw a wall, a wall, a wall and then there it was a door, a dusty old door! She almost squealed out loud with excitement.

"How silly, I should have thought of the door earlier. Of course, that's how the children get to us, how stupid of me. That's exactly the reason why I *must* get rid of fear; it puts a knot in my thinking cap every time."

A little further up the ladder she climbed, very careful not to wake Harry who was snoring his head off. She wanted to observe the large white door in more detail. At the bottom of the door was a long narrow slit; she began to feel very excited indeed, she was confident that crawling underneath would be possible. This zone became point B of her escape route.

Hurriedly she scurried down the ladder feeling positive and pleased. "I have no idea what's on the other side of the door, but I'll take the risk. Please dear Creator, protect and guide me and keep me safe from harm as I prepare to leap into the unknown."

Hennelie decided to make her get away that very night. Before leaving she would have to stock up on provisions for the journey, "Thank goodness for the pouches in my cheeks," she thought gratefully. Hennelie was always amazed at the amount of food that she could stuff away. Without dilly dallying she scurried to the food tray, hopped right into it and began to pack her cheeks to the brim.

"Hey! What do you think you are doing?" snarled a voice from above.

"Oh no, It's Harry, he's woken up!" Hennelie's heart pounded, her jaws froze and she sat quite still.

Her bulging cheeks made her look like she had the mumps.

"What a greedy, fat little guts you are," wheezed Harry nastily. "I suppose you were planning to gobble the lot and leave not a morsel for me, your loving *pardner!*" Harry always said his words wrong, there were so many things wrong about him.

He puffed himself out and came down the ladder slowly. He towered over Hennelie and hissed, "Just look at you." His eyes squinted, the look of disgust made his teeth protrude like a vampire hamster. He glared at her plump cheeks and like a spitting cobra he spat out, "you ugly undersized little stink bomb!"

In the past all the horrid names he used to call Hennelie would make her feel very upset. It wasn't fair. But today was different. Today she had hope. She was going to escape and it made Hennelie feel powerful inside, she didn't care what he said, she'd ignore him. She would not let him get to her.

Soon, very soon she would be leaving him behind, good riddance to bad rubbish. She saw him now so clearly for what he was, a pathetic, evil, spiteful bully, so unhappy within himself and his life that he took it out on her. "Bullies must be the worst creatures in the universe," thought Hennelie.

Harry realised that his nasty words were not affecting Hennelie as they used to. Why wasn't she flinching and cowering and looking down and pleading? She used to quiver and shake. Why wasn't she crying? His anger grew, his eyes began to pop out of their sockets, his vocal cords constricted and in a high pitched strangled voice he screamed out, "You pathetic little rat bag, I'll make you cry just see if I don't."

And with that he violently leapt onto Hennelie's back, knocking her sideways. He scratched and clawed at her, before sinking his razor sharp, pointed yellow teeth into her soft golden fur. The pain was excruciating. Tears sprung into her tightly clenched eyes. She squealed out and begged Harry to stop, but that only seemed to encourage him.

After what seemed like billions of hours of agony, he withdrew with a last hard bite into her neck. Hennelie dissolved into a heap of agonised sobs. Satisfied with her tears Harry puffed his chest out and began to wash himself vigorously ever so proud of himself for causing so much unhappiness. Hennelie slowly and painfully limped off to the opposite side of the cage. Her mouth was bone dry. She dragged her tiny body to the edge of the water tray and sipped thirstily.

Harry always developed a ferocious appetite after fighting with Hennelie. Biting into her soft flesh made his mouth water. So often he was tempted to devour her completely. But then, that would deprive him from the sheer delight of bullying her and watching her cry.

Out of the corner of her eye Hennelie watched Harry feast ravenously on half a boiled potato which had been put into the cage by the humans. Knowing him it would be quite a while before he stopped eating. She decided to stay crouched where she was and wait for him to eat. After that she knew he would return to his cubicle upstairs to sleep and that's when she'd make a run for it.

Curled up in a little furry ball exhaustion got the better of little Hennelie and by mistake she fell asleep. A couple of hours later she awoke with a jolt.

"Oh my gosh! What's the time? I hope I haven't over slept," she thought stricken with panic. She winced as she sat up hurriedly. Her tiny body ached all over from Harry's earlier attack. The memory of it reinforced her determination to get going immediately; there was no more time to waste.

She hastened to point A of her escape route plan, the gap in the cage. She stopped, looked, listened, to ensure there wasn't a murmur from Harry or any other creature in the house.

"Here goes," thought Hennelie bravely, "It's now or never." She thrust her small pink nose and face through the bars. She pushed hard, then hard again, until her whole head with the bulging cheeks popped through the bars. "Please fill me with your spirit; with your strength I know I can achieve the impossible," she prayed silently before she went on to twist forward, this way and that.

Suddenly one shoulder followed by the other was set free. "Push Hennelie, push!" she encouraged herself, "don't give up." It was her large tummy full of unborn babies that was causing most of the trouble.

She counted slowly to herself, "One, two, three..." she sucked in her breath, she sucked in her stomach and with all her might she strained, squeezed and pushed until phew! Out through the bars came her rounded stomach, her tiny legs and stubby tail. "I'm out, I'm out." Hennelie inwardly sang feeling very excited, "I'm out of the cage."

"Run, run, run," her voice inside urged. So over the grey cement floor Hennelie scampered as quickly as she could to the bottom of the large dusty white door, "and now to press myself down as flat as a pancake and slide under the door," she instructed herself. To Hennelie's amazement the slithering under the door was much easier than she had anticipated, and in no time at all she was through onto the other side. Standing on a soft pink carpet she panted with relief.

In front of her ran a long passage lined with shelves of books and she had a choice to make "Do I turn left or right?" all at once it became obvious that she had to make her way to a window. With her little heart racing, she thrust her tiny pink nose upward and sniffed, and sure enough her sensitive nose detected fresh air coming from the right hand side.

Without another thought she darted down the passage her whiskers rotating at high speed, until she came upon a green bedroom which contained three large windows invitingly sprawled across one wall.

With a thumping chest she scurried towards the old maroon rocking chair placed very conveniently beneath one of the windows. She clawed her way up the knobbly fabric until she balanced on the headrest which very fortunately was touching the window sill.

"Oh dear, the windows are covered with gauze to keep mosquitoes out." Hennelie experienced a wave of disappointment. "Buck up Hennelie. Don't give in to negative thoughts. Remember your nice sharp teeth. Gnaw your way through the gauze." The inner voice saved her every time and reminded her once again that fear and panic simply stopped clear thinking.

Hennelie gnawed and gnawed until she had made a decent enough hole for her little body to pass through.

For a minute she stood quite still. The fresh evening air was heavenly, intoxicating. Hennelie sighed, "This is magic; the smell of the crisp night air, the smell of the wet earth after the rain, the smell of freedom."

Dreamily she looked upward and saw the beauty of the stars and the great majestic full moon.

Thank heavens for her inner voice which gave her a nudge bringing her back to reality by reminding her of her mission. Yes, she had better get a move on and be on the alert for old mean cats. They were plentiful. She had heard them meowing around and about often enough. She shivered at the thought of them.

"Quickly jump down off the window sill onto the grass beneath, it looks thick and long and should make for a soft landing," she said to herself. And without further ado she shut her eyes tightly and leapt into the darkness with nothing but trust and faith in her Creator; a feeling so steadfast and secure in her heart and soul.

Plop. She landed safely. The wet dewy grass had cushioned her fall perfectly.

Suddenly to her left she heard soft clucking sounds, hen sounds. She knew what hens were from her time in the pet shop. She had always liked these creatures. She knew they were no threat. "I'm sure they'll be able to advise me in which direction I should travel," she thought, relief flooding through her as she crept carefully and quietly to the small hen house.

Whispering softly Hennelie said, "Excuse me," then a little louder, "*Excuse me,* is anyone awake?" cluck, cluck, puk, puk. The hens became restless.

Hennelie whispered quickly, "Sssh, please don't make a noise."

"Who's there?" a hen clucked back fiercely.

"It's only me, Hennelie Hamster, I need your help please," pleaded Hennelie.

The hens clicked their beaks crossly, "You should not creep up on us like that, especially since we've been living on our nerves of late in fear of Wild Cat. He's a serial killer and he's been on the prowl around here. He comes from the hills. We are easy prey for him cooped up in here, cluck cluck!"

Wild Cat. The news hit Hennelie like an electric current. All cats were bad news and a terrible threat to her and she began to tremble.

"What are you doing out here at night, its not safe, go back to where you came from," said one of the hens.

"What a terrible risk you are taking, you'll never make it. Go back," said another.

All Hennelie's doubts began to re-surface. Perhaps she was being foolish taking this chance, perhaps she was better off in the cage with Harry. Was her dream of living free in the wilderness just a load of unrealistic mumbo jumbo, and impossible for a mere hamster to accomplish? Her thoughts, feelings and brain waves started to spin, she felt as if she was heading for a convulsion.

In a shaky thin voice she said, "I'm so sorry, I never meant to scare you, and I had no idea about the… the…." Hennelie couldn't utter the name of the ferocious creature, she was so terrified.

A hen began to gently sob, "We have lost so many of our dear friends."

Another hen added, "The farmer and his wife have tried many times to shoot beastly Wild Cat but the wily creature seems to get away every time."

Hennelie was now reduced to a ball of quivering fur. Her former courage and determination had disappeared in a flash, and fear once again reared its ugly head making her feel weak and helpless.

"Go, please just go. For your own safety," a hen warned.

"Go? Go where?" Hennelie thought, suddenly confused and filled with panic.

Thank goodness, for her inner voice or was it the voice of her Creator which came to her rescue yet again with sensible advice amidst her turmoil. "Keep calm, breathe deeply. Keep going forward. Press on, Hennelie. Don't lose hope. Remember your vision, visualise it, see it clearly in your mind. Believe in yourself. Do not turn back. Have courage Hennelie. You can do it. Have faith."

Of course, there was no going back. Hennelie knew this. She took a deep breath and silently and very seriously asked of her Creator, "Please, please help me to keep moving forward. Help me achieve my dream. Help me to shake off fear, and please give me renewed strength."

Hennelie put her shoulders back, "Yes you're right I must go," she said to the hens, "but I'm not altogether sure how to get out of this courtyard. Could you please point me in the right direction?"

"She's crazy," clucked a hen.

"She'll never make it," clucked another.

Hennelie decided not to listen to their words of doom and gloom. Instead she chose to trust her instincts, to trust the good positive feelings deep inside.

A sympathetic hen told Hennelie that if she travelled directly southwards, she would get to a small black wrought iron gate, which seemed to be the only way out. Before dashing off at great speed Hennelie thanked the hens and said she would ask the Creator to grant them protection from Wild Cat.

"Creator? What Creator?" clucked a hen.

"Who the heck is the Creator?" clucked another.

"She must be a bit bonkers, poor creature! The lights are on but no one's at home! Tut tut cluck," said a hen.

The run across the courtyard was the spookiest thing Hennelie had ever experienced. Nasty visions of Wild Cat stalking her fuelled her imagination. Visions of sharp teeth and claws tormented her. "Control your thoughts," reminded her inner voice. "Don't let the negative forces hinder you. You are making good progress, keep going. Keep calm."

After what seemed an eternity, Hennelie arrived at the black gate. Once again relief flooded through her tiny frame. She stood panting and saturated from the icy grass at the bottom of it. "Keep going, don't stop," she urged herself. So she scurried through the wrought iron bars of the gate as fast as she could.

A light drizzle started to fall and Hennelie was thankful for it. She was feeling so hot and flushed from that scary run across the courtyard. She crouched behind a pile of rubble to catch her breath. After a short time she felt much calmer; her breathing became more regulated. She welcomed the tender droplets which fell gently and soothingly upon her furry golden back, bringing her back to her senses.

With her tiny pink paws she rubbed her little face over and over again, in a desperate attempt to wash away all the bad memories of the life she had just left behind.

Suddenly, the most fearsome sound reverberated in the darkness, "Woof, woof, woof!" Hennelie almost jumped out of her fur. Without thinking she dashed out from behind the rubble, ran this way and that and back behind the pile of stones, "What was that?" her whiskers twitched frantically.

Very slowly and cautiously she peered out from her hiding place, and there to her amazement she saw standing in a row three black and white hairy creatures with long noses, long tails and large pointed ears, she gasped, "What are those?" She looked at them long and hard and wondered whether these were friend or foe.

"There's only one way to find out," she thought bravely, "I will call out to them and see how they react. Excuse me," she called out politely, but there was no response. She cleared her throat, took a deep breath and shouted, *"Excuse me."* The creatures' ears pricked up, their heads lifted up and sideways suspiciously and a deep gruff growling sound rumbled in a throat.

"Please don't be angry," Hennelie pleaded, "My name is Hennelie Hamster; I am very small and can do you no harm."

The biggest of the three sounding very much like a policeman barked, "What are you doing out here?"

Hennelie said in a small little voice that she was running away from a very unhappy life. She explained what her life had been like in the cage with Harry. She mentioned that she was expecting babies and she wanted a better future for them and herself, and that she would rather die than to see her children living in a cage as she had done at the mercy of bullies. She said simply, "I want to find freedom and I believe it is out there somewhere."

Listening to Hennelie's story made the creatures' hearts melt. Their tails dropped and they didn't seem so furious. The big one coughed and asked gruffly "Where are you?"

"I'm here behind the rubble," Hennelie answered before asking, "Is it safe for me to come out?"

"Of course you may come out, we will not harm you," said one of the black and white creatures.

Hennelie slowly appeared, "Here I am." She looked so tiny and vulnerable.

The creatures looked about in all directions, confused.

"I'm very small," she said. "I'm here on the ground in front of you." She stood on her little back legs so they could see her better.

Only then did they spot her. They moved closer sniffing, "Ah," one said knowingly, "you're a rat."

"No, I am not a rat," said Hennelie crossly, "I'm a hamster."

"A hamster? What is a hamster?"

"I am a hamster! We are very different to rats but I'm not going into all that now," she muttered. Pride had almost got the better of her. She was just about to say something derogatory about rats but stopped herself just in time.

She knew it wasn't fair to judge other creatures and put oneself above them. Every living creature had the right to be here on earth, and each had a purpose. There was a reason and a special plan for everything.

It reminded Hennelie of a time in the pet shop, when a lady from England was explaining to the shop keeper that people in England hated creatures called pigeons and squirrels, because they would eat all the wild bird seeds out in the garden.

To Hennelie it didn't seem fair to feed some creatures and not others. The injustice of it; why were certain creatures unloved and looked down upon? Not fair at all.

The three creatures in front of her looked disappointed that she wasn't going to elaborate further on the differences between hamsters and rats. They so enjoyed a bit of gossip and a belittling of others now and again, a good laugh at another creature's expense.

Hennelie decided she would entertain them instead with the little she knew about hamsters. "Okay, okay, what I understand is that we hamsters are originally from Syria, which is somewhere or other in the universe, and when humans first saw us many years ago they decided to keep us caged up as pets for their amusement. Our ancestors were carried off to different countries; our families were broken up, our communities destroyed, and now we are spread all over the world, all separated from one another.

"Mm interesting, now tell us what you know about rats."

"Sorry I don't know enough about rats I'm afraid," she said and changed the subject quickly. "May I ask what you three creatures are?" she twitched her whiskers with interest.

"Us," they chorused together before howling with laughter, "We are dogs! Border collies to be precise! Some humans call us sheep dogs. Our real purpose in life is to round up sheep, but alas, there are no sheep on this farm, so we end up barking up the wrong tree most of the time. We chase the cows instead, but it's not the same," the big one said looking a little melancholy.

"It's naughty really," said the small one, "but we get so bored."

"Do you have individual names?" Hennelie asked.

"Oh yes," piped up the smallest of the three, "of course we do – I am Sally, that is Rip and this is Rocky."

"Well I'm very pleased to meet you," said Hennelie happily, "I only wish we had longer to get to know each other better, but I really should be getting on my way. You see us hamsters usually sleep during the daytime and become active at night because we are nocturnal creatures. By morning I will be absolutely exhausted so I'll need a safe place to rest by then and looking at the position of the moon I see I have no time to waste. It won't be long before it grows light."

Hennelie rubbed her face quickly before asking shyly, "Would it be too much of an imposition to ask if perhaps you three dogs could put me on the right path? I'm not really sure of the way forward from here."

"I'm not a dog," said the smaller one sulkily, "I'm a bitch." And they all burst into barking laughter again.

The big handsome dog called Rip said apologetically, "Please excuse her Hennelie dear. Sally is just teasing you. But she is quite right, female dogs are actually called bitches and the males are called dogs. It was my mistake when I introduced us all as dogs, sorry Sal."

Sally wagged her tail impishly.

"Well, I think we'd better get a move on if we are going to help Hennelie find her way," said Rocky also wagging his long hairy tail, "come along."

Hennelie set off down the garden path with three cheerful, handsome and strong escorts at her side.

The beauty of the garden took Hennelie's breath away. Highlighting from the full moon on the dewy foliage and blooms in the darkness created a celestial effect.

She couldn't help but notice the artistry of the bold blood red bougainvillea creepers, how they intertwined with the tall trees whilst others languished exotically over the wall. In the beds of red earth, between large clumps of fluffy pampas grass, dazzling faces of busy lizzies smiled upwards with eyes closed toward the moon beams. Trailing on either side contentedly, tumbled orange flowery plants which Sally explained were called nasturtiums. Here and there daisy bushes, agapanthus and strelitzias, swayed in the cool breeze. A row of pink and blue hydrangeas leaned against the wall and looked on.

"Why not stay and rest awhile so that you can see the garden in the daylight Hennelie? By day it's truly the most exquisite sight to behold," said Rocky.

"I'm sure it must be," replied Hennelie regretfully. "I would love more than anything to see the garden in the sunshine, but I'm so afraid of being captured and caged again by the humans, or pounced on by Wild Cat. I just feel it's better for me to make a clean getaway as far from the house and garden as possible. I'm sure everybody will be on the hunt for me in the morning."

Rip and Sally agreed with Hennelie.

Further down the path, Hennelie exclaimed, "Oh what a glorious aroma." She stopped to take a deep breath.

"That comes from the blue, lilac and white flowers on those bushes. I've heard the humans call them yesterday, today and tomorrow bushes. Their lovely lingering smell seems to be more prominent by night," said Sally.

Hennelie sighed, "I can't tell you how marvellous I feel." She stood on her little back legs and rubbed her face again. "Am I really out of the cage? Or am I dreaming?"

"No, you're not dreaming little Hennelie," replied Sally moving closer to her lovingly, protectively. "You're definitely not dreaming."

There was a moment's silence just then, each creature lost in their own thoughts, dreaming their own dreams.

The shrill cry of the nightjar jolted them back to reality. "Have you got your breath back Hennelie?" asked Rocky kindly. Hennelie smiled and nodded.

"It's not far to the security gate now," said Rip encouragingly.

"Another gate?" asked Hennelie with a certain weariness in her voice, "I wonder how many I shall have to pass through in my lifetime?"

Each walked the rest of the way in silence.

When Hennelie stopped again it was in front of a great, big, enormous security gate, which loomed up almost to the sky. It was locked and bolted with a huge brass padlock.

Hennelie was taken aback, "Why on earth would the humans lock themselves in a cage?" she asked shocked.

"For protection," said Rip, "they too live with fear. They fight amongst each other," he said matter of factly.

Sally giggled frivolously, "Every creature wants to be top dog I guess."

"Not every creature, I don't," said Hennelie seriously. "I just want to be free and happy and content and to fulfil my purpose in life; and of course to live without fear is high on my agenda."

"I wonder if that's possible in this day and age," said Rip thoughtfully.

"These days it's dog eat dog," Sally barked and giggled. The others chose to ignore her. You could tell she was the joker of the pack.

"I think it is possible Rip," said Hennelie, "with the help of our Creator; he can help us conquer fear and achieve true peace, love and everlasting joy. Without his help I don't think it's really possible to tell the truth."

"Yes I feel that too," said Sally seriously for once.

"But where is he, this Creator?" said Rocky.

"He is all around. If you talk to him, and listen carefully, you will hear him," said Hennelie, "I personally don't question and argue and debate and doubt, like the other creatures in the pet shop used to do. I just feel deep down that he is there and that he is on my side. It is a very comforting feeling. I simply believe and trust and have faith. I keep talking to him and his voice comes back to me every time a little bit louder. I think it was my loneliness and unhappiness which brought me close to him. He was my only friend. A friend I can't do without now. I would never dare do what I am doing without his help. I need him. I am too small to take these big dreams on by myself. I know with him behind me all things are possible. I will simply trust in him. I wish we could talk more about it but I really need to be getting along."

"You are an inspiration Hennelie," said Sally genuinely, "you have really given us food for thought. I admire you so much for your courage."

"Hennelie dear, this is where we must say goodbye. As much as we'd like to, we are not free to go with you any further. You at least are small enough to slip through the wire mesh," said Rip tenderly. "Being small has its advantages."

Tears welled up in Hennelie's tiny black eyes. She rubbed them away quickly with her tiny paws and bit her lip to stop herself from crying. In a soft choked up little voice she said, "I can't tell you how much I appreciate what you have done for me," she trailed off as her voice became stuck in her throat and she rubbed her eyes again.

"Go Hennelie, you're free now. May the Creator be with you on your journey," said Sally gently nudging her on.

These four creatures had known each other for such a short time, yet this moment of parting brought such sadness for all concerned. These were Hennelie's first real creature friends. They had been so kind to her and now she was leaving them behind. She looked at them a last time and noticed how their heads hung and their tails drooped.

All she could utter was a tiny simple "thank you" which she meant from the bottom of her breaking heart before turning sharply to dart through the security gate.

CROSSROADS

It was beginning to grow light. Hennelie couldn't believe the magnificence of the early morning sky. The beauty at break of day made hot tears prick at her eyes. This was the first time she had ever seen it.

Standing on her back legs, clasping her tiny pink paws she gazed at the sky. What a perfect picture, it was breath-taking. Pink, purple, grey and pale blue spread across the horizon. "It's a miracle," Hennelie breathed softly. She would have stood there for hours if it hadn't been for the cockerel sounding his trumpet with a loud *Cock a Doodle Doo!*

"Oh dear, I'd better hurry along," thought Hennelie, "soon the household will be up and about; they'll notice my absence which will most definitely be followed by a hamster hunt."

A pigeon cooed and all at once the silence of the garden was broken by the dawn chorus. A sound which was to Hennelie's ears pure delight. A harmonious melody, of chirruping, whistling, tweeting, clucking and crowing.

Sprawled out in front of her was a wide sandy farm road which contained several puddles.

It was the Christmas season, a time when there was generally a lot of rain in Zimbabwe; hot, humid, clear blue skies one minute and frightening electrical storms the next. At least for now last night's drizzle had stopped.

The land in front of her was quite different from the garden. It went on and on untamed all about. Looking at it spread out mile upon mile made Hennelie's little legs start shaking, "Can I really do this?" she questioned herself. This of course was a big mistake; fear thrived on self doubt. The taunting started all over again. "Good question Hennelie, can you take that lot on? You being so small and all, what are you going to eat out there?"

"Do not listen. Stay focused. Don't look too far ahead. Do what you can today. Tackle the crossroad first, and then little by little you can take on the rest. It *is* possible. Stay positive." Her inner voice spoke encouragingly.

She closed her eyes quickly, "Dear Creator, is that you talking?" Before she could go on she felt something brush up against her bottom. She let out an almighty yelp and almost collapsed in a heap with fright.

"Hey," purred a sultry voice, "what's your problem? Got ants in your pants?"

Hennelie turned quickly her heart racing, and came face to face with the weirdest, oddest, creepy crawly she had ever seen. Her mouth flew open; her eyes grew wide, "Just look at all those legs." She thought awe struck.

The look on her face made the creature chuckle. He came towards her legs and feet rippling, feelers wriggling energetically. "My apologies for giving you such a turn," he said with a smirk. "I'm afraid my eyesight is not very good at the best of times. Now my dear who might you be?"

Hennelie stuttered and stammered, "Oh...Um...I'm Hennelie Hamster," she replied awkwardly.

"How do you do? And I'm Charles, Charles Chongololo, very pleased to meet you."

Hennelie felt very embarrassed and ashamed of herself for not hiding her astonishment at his strange appearance more successfully.

"I'm sorry, Charles, but my nerves are slightly frayed at the moment. Morning has broken and I must get across the road as quickly as possible to find shelter and a safe place to nap. You see hamsters, which is what I am, stay up all night and by the time morning comes find ourselves totally exhausted."

"I quite understand," said Charles pleasantly. "I would escort you over the road but unfortunately we chongololos are very slow on our feet. It would therefore be risky for us both. But, my dear, I am very skilled at sensing approaching vehicles from the vibrations they emit as they travel down the road."

"Let me demonstrate." His feelers twisted and twirled expertly like a sort of alien radar, until he said with satisfaction, "right this minute, seems perfectly safe to me. Permit me to suggest you make a dash for it immediately my dear."

"Wow! That's remarkable Charles, what a marvellous gift you have," Hennelie said gratefully. She was mighty impressed by the professional way in which he handled the safety issue of her crossing. What a perfect gentleman she thought.

Charles seemed pleased with the compliment. As soon as they had bid farewell to one another he curled up smartly in a small black neat coil.

Between the puddles Hennelie scurried, over sharp pointy stones she sped. When she had almost reached the other side of the road, a loud, highly threatening revving sound rumbled aggressively somewhere nearby. She stopped dead in her tracks.

Charles in the meantime had detected the vibrations from where he was and in lightening speed he swiftly uncurled himself and screeched in an ultra high pitched siren like chongololo voice, "Run Hennelie, run! It's coming towards you. It's a tractor. Run Hennelie."

Without thinking Hennelie took a running jump, and nose dived head first into a clump of wet grass.

She squeezed her eyes tight as a tractor and trailer roared passed only inches from her short stubby tail. "Phew! That was a close shave." Hennelie panted as she slowly disentangled her furry body from the matted grass.

"Are you alright?" Charles shouted anxiously.

Hennelie felt sick. What a terrible fright she had got. She slowly managed to turn around to shout back across the road, "I'm fine Charles, just fine," before all went black.

A couple of hours went by before Hennelie awoke. She would've gone on sleeping had it not been for the loud deep throated "Moo" that echoed in her ears.

Still a tiny bit dazed she sprung up hastily, "What was that?" She was having difficulty focusing on anything as one of her eyes was gummed together with sleep. Very quickly she licked her tiny pink paws and rubbed her eyes until her vision returned to normal. "That's better, now what was that noise?"

Suddenly the biggest brown face emerged out of the long grass and dipped down next to her. Hennelie tried to run, she tried to scream, but found she couldn't move a muscle. She realized then that her body had gone into shock.

The creature opened its pink mouth, flicked out a pink tongue and wrapped it around a tuft of green grass. There was a tug, a snap and a munching, crunching sound as its jaws rotated slowly, grinding and crushing blades of grass methodically.

The beast looked at her blankly with glazed, uncaring, glassy eyes, whilst she stood rooted to the spot. Hennelie watched the creature fearfully and suspiciously from where she was, and noticed that all it seemed to do was eat and eat and swish its wiry tail to and fro to keep green flies off its buxom buttocks. She caught sight of four legs with knobbly knees which amazingly held up an enormous brown barrel of a body.

"What are you staring at?" the creature mumbled irritably over a mouthful of grass.

The words broke the ice. All at once Hennelie's fear seemed to evaporate. "I'm sorry, I know that it's very rude to stare," said Hennelie, slightly shaken, "please forgive me. Let me introduce myself. I'm Hennelie Hamster, and I'm sorry to have disrupted your meal."

"Oh nonsense," the creature said moodily, "nothing disturbs my meals except those idiotic border collies when they are let out of the garden gate. Such undisciplined creatures. There are no sheep on the farm so they insist on taking out their frustrations on us girls by chasing us all over the paddock. What they need is a good kick up their rumps." The creature said with disgust.

"Oh dear that's a bit harsh, those are my new friends," thought Hennelie. "I don't mean to be rude, but what sort of creature are you?" asked Hennelie.

"I'm a heifer," the creature droned indifferently, "heifer meaning young female cow that hasn't had any calves yet, or kids, brats, babies whatever you like to call them," she continued chewing lazily. "Anyway I'm off now; it's time for me to look for greener pastures. The grass always seems to look greener on the other side so that's where I'm heading. Good day to you Miss Mouse!"

"Huh! What a nerve calling me Miss Mouse," Hennelie thought miffed and was about to say something but the hefty creature had already sauntered off.

"Oh, just as well," she decided with a sigh, sometimes it was better to leave things unsaid. "Always try and walk away from trouble," was what the pet shop owner always told his volatile wife. Advice that she never adhered to, and then wondered why she was always in a scrap with either the Zimbabwean law or some other human being, which caused bad feelings all round.

Hennelie hadn't eaten for hours and hours. Luckily she had the stored away nuts and seeds in the pouches of her cheeks. She couldn't wait to tuck in, but first she had to find a nice safe place to hide.

A little way off lay an abandoned irrigation pipe, "Oh yippee!" thought Hennelie gleefully, "I'll crawl inside; it'll be an ideal hiding place. Pipes are usually nice and cool. I'll have a nibble and a nap and wait for the day to cool down." And into the dark irrigation pipe she scurried.

A crack of lightening, a rumble of thunder and Hennelie was awake in a flash. She had been curled up in the pipe since mid-morning, enjoying a deep undisturbed, well earned snooze. She felt energised and much stronger. There was nothing better than a good sleep. She stretched her front legs, then her back legs. Her body felt free from all the earlier aches and pains and her paws no longer felt tender. All was good.

She peeped out of the pipe. It was early evening. Hennelie always felt far sprightlier at this time of the day. She thrust her little nose to the wind, "Rain is on its way, I must hurry." The last thing she needed was to get caught in a storm. In the distance she could see a white building. She decided to head for it without delay.

The going was rough and tough, the grass was very spikey and long which slowed her scurrying down quite a lot.

You could tell there had been a lot of rain about, the earth was saturated, "I mustn't get stuck in the mud," Hennelie thought and she began to chant, "keep to the high ground, keep to the dry ground, keep to the high ground, keep to the dry ground..."

This kept her mind busy in a positive way to ensure that no negative forces could intrude and put her off her stride. Carefully she zigzagged through the mire.

Under a wooden fence she scampered, over some mushy leaves she tramped, over protruding roots of towering trees she clambered, until finally, only a stone's throw away was the white building. "Oh, thank goodness," she panted relieved, "almost there." With an energetic spurt she sped to the bottom of a large wooden door where she discovered with delight that a generous chunk of wood was missing from the left hand corner.

"What an ideal entrance for a hamster to creep through; and my goodness what a delicious, mouth watering smell," Hennelie thought. Her nose twitched appreciatively. After blinking a couple of times her eyes became accustomed to the darkness.

She tiptoed further into the room. A sniff here and snuffle there and in no time at all she had located where the highly satisfactory smell was coming from.

In a bulky hessian sack was the most ginormous supply of food. She scurried up the bulbous heap and at the top she discovered to her sheer delight, zillions of cubes of tantalizing titbits. "Manna from heaven" Hennelie wanted to shout and jump and leap about with joy. Instead because she was so famished she got stuck into the mound right away.

What ever it was, it was deliriously delicious. She nibbled and nibbled, at times with her eyes closed to savour the phenomenally fabulous flavour, until her little tummy was full and round and her cheeks stuffed to the brim with extra rations for the road.

Whilst she licked her lips after her scrumptious meal she suddenly felt little kicks and movements in her tummy from the babies. Hennelie smiled. She was so excited to have her babies; she couldn't wait to have a family to take care of and to love. She knew she must be patient.

She still had a long way to travel; she needed to reach the far distant hills in the north where she would be free from the humans forever. Free to raise her little family, free to create a community perhaps, or a new hamster colony eventually.

As she cleaned her face with her tiny paws she wondered where all these ideas and ambitions of hers had come from. Who had planted this feeling inside her? An unrelenting need to fulfil some sort of purpose; a burning desire that never subsided, was it the Creator? Or was it simply delusions of grandeur? How could one so small have such huge dreams? Sometimes, she felt quite befuddled by it all; yet the voice within never ceased, "Keep going. Keep trying. Victory waits."

The scrumptious meal made Hennelie feel frisky indeed. She scurried down the sack to explore her new surroundings. She poked her little face outside the door. Night time had arrived. "The best time of the day," Hennelie sighed blissfully.

The birds were tucked up in their nests; the stars twinkled in the sky and the moon glowed brightly all around.

To her right Hennelie spotted two more wooden doors. She couldn't resist popping into the one closest to her. As she did so pointy bits of hay poked at her undercarriage "Ouch!" she winced. *Suddenly* her whiskers went on edge, her built in alarm system alerted her to another presence in the room which was confirmed by a snort and a heavy thudding stamp.

She tumbled backwards with fright and fell hard against a rough cement trough. High pitched whinnying laughter burst forth from what looked like two heifers, one black and the other brown.

Hennelie was furious, "It's not funny," she shrilled angrily, "it's downright nasty to laugh at somebody when they fall, you two heifers should know better." This made the creatures laugh even more. They shook their heads and stamped their feet whinnying uncontrollably. Hennelie was near to tears, "I knew heifers were rude, but not that rude and unkind." She complained feeling hurt. Her sad little face brought an end to the hysterical laughter. She looked so tiny and helpless standing beside the water trough rubbing her face.

"Oh dear we didn't mean to upset you," said the black one sheepishly, "It's just that you called us heifers when we are in actual fact horses."

Hennelie's brows wrinkled in confusion, "Horses?"

"Yes, we are horses. I am Monty and my dear companion here is Mon Cherie. Welcome to our stable."

Hennelie's nose and ears turned quite red, "How silly of me, I'm sorry, it's just that I met a heifer earlier in the day and I thought…well, I thought that perhaps you were one and the same," she said cringing.

"Oh please think nothing more of it," said Mon Cherie kindly, "now please do tell us what you're doing in this neck of the woods. We haven't seen you around these parts before."

"It's a long story," said Hennelie, "I'll tell you about it, but before I do would you mind very much if I had a sip of your water, I'm parched."

"Please help yourself," neighed Monty generously, "and how about a bite to eat? We have plenty of food here so please do help yourself."

"Crikey, I've done that already in the adjoining room," thought Hennelie guiltily.

"Ah that's better. I was feeling very thirsty, thank you." Hennelie hurriedly washed her face with her tiny paws. Boy, she couldn't wait to give her whole well-travelled body a good wash. How she hated being dirty, which she certainly was after that long haul in the mud.

The horses watched and waited patiently to hear her story. This couple had always been interested in other creatures' experiences. They genuinely loved others and believed each creature had a wonderful story to tell about their lives.

Hennelie hopped down off the trough, ran across the hay, and climbed up onto the black treated poles that divided their two sections equally. As she stood on the top pole she was able to look the two directly in the eye. With good eye contact it was much easier to communicate. Clearing her throat Hennelie related the story of her escape from the cage and the farm house. "And when I discovered that I was going to have babies I decided to run away." She added finally.

"Babies, Oh Divine," whinnied Mon Cherie delightedly. "Makorokoto! as the rural folk say in Shona."

"Makorokoto means congratulations in English. Shona is the language spoken by the farm labourers," explained Monty merrily looking at Hennelie's confused face. "Oh, what perfectly lovely news," he neighed.

There was great excitement in the stable for quite a while.

When all had calmed down, Hennelie went on to describe the minute details of her escape, to the amazement of the two attentive horses who whinnied and neighed with incredible disbelief at appropriate intervals.

"How brave." Mon Cherie snorted in admiration for the tiny figure she saw in front of her. "Very courageous," agreed Monty sincerely.

Ending on a happy note Hennelie told of all the wonderful creatures she had so far met along the way. "And now here I am with you horses, my two new friends."

The three of them continued to chat and swop stories and experiences throughout the night, sipping on water, nibbling on the odd horse cube, until the early hours of the next morning, when Hennelie heard to her horror the sound of human footsteps.

"Don't panic," whispered Monty calmly, "it's only Alfons the stable hand. He's come to open the doors to let us out into the paddock to graze."

"Hide behind the water trough he won't see you there," said Mon Cherie.

Hurriedly Hennelie scrambled down the poles as fast as she could and across to the water trough. Just then the stable doors were unbolted one by one and the horses ambled out into the paddock as if nothing had happened. The footsteps retreated and all was peaceful once again.

Hennelie decided to stay near the water trough and give herself that much needed wash. Expertly she licked her tiny paws, rubbed her face, wiped behind her ears, scrubbed her round tummy, her sides and under her legs, two or three times until she was satisfied that she was scrupulously clean.

Hamsters are fanatical about cleanliness and hygiene, which is probably one of the reasons why humans enjoyed keeping them as pets.

She gave a big stretch. There was nothing better than being spotless and well fed. How happy and blessed she felt, "Now to join my two new friends in the paddock."

Hennelie scurried to the door, looked left and right, and dashed over the cement quad and out into the paddock where Monty and Mon Cherie stood waiting for her.

"Ah good, there you are." said Monty, "and looking very spick and span too," he added with a wink.

"Oh yes," said Hennelie coquettishly, "thought I'd spruce up for my two new friends." She loved the light hearted banter she shared with Monty and Mon Cherie. They always seemed to be laughing and joking. It was such fun to be with them. Monty was just about to crack another of his jokes when a chilling shrill pierced the jovial atmosphere.

In a flash there was a swoop, a flutter and another stabbing screech, "It's a hawk," Mon Cherie whinnied wildly. "A hawk!"

It was all too fast. All Hennelie could remember was Mon Cherie rearing up formidably on her hind legs and lashing out ruthlessly with her front legs at the enemy, which was a sleek, yellow eyed, razor beaked bird of prey, which possessed the sharpest claws that Hennelie had ever seen. There was a thudding collision of hooves and wings, an ear piercing screech and silence as the large bird hightailed it back to the sky.

The three creatures stood stunned in disbelief at what had just taken place. When reality dawned Hennelie broke down and sobbed uncontrollably. Had it not been for her friends Hennelie knew that her journey would've been over.

The two horses felt angry at themselves for their carelessness. They had seen the hawk before at the stables, "How could we have been so stupid and reckless?" stamped Monty, "we very nearly had Hennelie killed."

"Oh Hennelie please forgive us," said Mon Cherie. Hennelie was finding great difficulty in curbing her gushing tears. "I think we should get you back to the stable. You've had a terrible shock. You need to lie down and get your strength back."

Sleeping was exactly what Hennelie felt like doing. That nasty incident had robbed her of every last ounce of energy.

The horrible experience set her off again thinking too far ahead and this was dangerous. Suddenly everything seemed too much, the future seemed too overwhelming.

How was she going to survive on her own? Perhaps she should have a re-think and settle here with the horses to protect her. There was food, shelter, good company. What more could she wish for. The forces of darkness had set to work preparing to rob her of her vision, of her joy, of her mission. A mishap such as this presented the perfect opportunity for them to attack.

"I don't think I can go on," Hennelie mumbled between sobs, as the two horses escorted her back to the stable.

They watched the small creature sadly from the door until she had settled herself at the back of Mon Cherie's stable under some warm hay. "Thank you for saving my life," Hennelie whispered weakly from where she was before slipping off to sleep.

Which wasn't really a sleep at all; it was more like a torture chamber full of the most horrific nightmares. Poor little Hennelie was wracked with evil visions of being snatched high into the sky by sharp claws which pierced her belly full of unborn children. Fear of the worst kind gripped her. She twisted and turned beneath the hay, her body ached. She dreamed of blood and gore. She dreamed of deformed children starving in the wilderness. She dreamed of suffocating in the mud.

On and on the torture continued until she awoke exhausted, to the clip clopping of hooves on the cement slab outside the stable. Instead of waking up refreshed as she normally did, she felt tired and depressed.

The two horses were encouraged into the stable by Alfons who served up a delicious dinner of horse cubes, molasses, bran and fresh water. This evening, Hennelie didn't care if Alfons saw her, she felt so weary. She began to think she'd be better off dead, or back in the cage.

The incident had robbed her of her energy and enthusiasm. It had left her doubting that she had the ability to accomplish her dreams. It had knocked her off her pedestal. She just felt like giving up. Her bright future suddenly seemed so unattainable and too hard to achieve.

The bolts were shut, the footsteps disappeared and the night had come. The three creatures were alone again. The atmosphere was glum. Hennelie was usually such a bright little spark but tonight it seemed the stuffing had gone out of her, even her fur looked drab. It usually shone a lovely golden colour.

Hennelie Hamster Running Wild • 49

"My dear you really must put the incident out of your mind. It's all over now, you are safe. You have so much to look forward to," said Mon Cherie in a motherly way.

"Yes get back on the horse, so to speak," said Monty gruffly.

"I know what you mean," said Hennelie limply, "but suddenly I don't think I've got what it takes. My dreams are too big; I'm too small, too weak. I'm not acquainted with the bush, I'm not very clever, I'm....."

"You are *stronger* than you think you are Hennelie. And please stop saying disrespectful things about yourself. It's not fair to downgrade yourself like that. Look back on what you've achieved so far - you escaped the cage, the humans, the cats, the tractor, the hawk. Those are huge accomplishments. Don't let today's incident stop you from going on. You have a destiny to fulfil." said Mon Cherie firmly.

"Do you really think so?" asked Hennelie.

"Of course I think so. I know so. You have come too far to give up now. You must start to believe in yourself again. Be kind to yourself. Give yourself a pat on the back. You are brave, you have courage, and you are gifted. Not to continue to strive and go forward would be such a waste Hennelie dear. Please you must believe me, you must keep on with your dreams, you cannot give up now," said Mon Cherie passionately.

"Do you believe in the Creator?" asked Hennelie softly.

"Yes we certainly do," said Mon Cherie with conviction, "and that goes for both me and Monty. We have come a long way with the Creator's help. You see we are both from Animal Rescue. Prior to that I cannot go into, it's too painful to recall, except to tell you that it was hell on earth. We were both ill treated and our spirits crushed. Our faith restored us, and it is that faith which has brought us to where we are today. At last we have found happiness; and by our Creator's grace Monty and I are still together, we were so very nearly separated."

"But how did you learn about the Creator?" asked Hennelie.

"We heard his voice and paid attention to it in our desperate times. We always felt his presence. We couldn't help but lean on him, he was our only hope," replied Mon Cherie.

"Some creatures hear the voice but refuse to acknowledge it," added Monty.

Gradually Hennelie began to relax and regain her old spirit. No one dared to bring the hawk subject up. Instead they shared the nice juicy dinner and talked about the future. The horses remained positive about it and their ideas and words began to rekindle the fire within Hennelie, stirring up her passion, renewing excitement and giving her hope once again.

"Dust yourself off and start all over again." Monty encouraged with a gutsy snort.

They went on to chat about Hennelie's little babies that were due soon, "Oh I do hope we get to meet them someday," sighed Mon Cherie, "what a beautiful Christmas gift for you Hennelie," she added warmly.

Before they knew it, morning had arrived; the cockerels and birds took it upon themselves to alert *Recondite Farm.*

Soon Alfons would arrive to let the horses out to graze, but before he did Hennelie wanted to tell the horses that last night's talk had made her feel so much better. She felt stronger thanks to them. She was ready to move on. Hennelie had decided to leave them later on in the day. She told them that she had managed to shake off the negative fiends that had tried to trap and curse her, thanks to their wise counsel. She thanked them for inspiring her with their stories. "It just goes to show how easy it is to lose one's balance. Any obstacle or mishap can so quickly throw one off course." Hennelie told them she had learnt a great lesson.

She knew that from now on every bit of her strength would be needed to fight the demons. The road would be tough, but she had to weather the storms with every ounce of faith, to get to her final destination just as they had done.

Hennelie knew failure to continue on her mission would mean a life incomplete and unfulfilled. Broken dreams would haunt and terrorise her throughout her life and lead to unhappiness.

Last night Mon Cherie had said, "There is treasure in the trails." Hennelie decided to hang on tightly to those words and just keep going come rain or shine.

With happy memories of her two dear friends, Hennelie left the stables as the afternoon began to draw to a close and headed north, straight for the kopjes in the distance.

THE BUSHVELD

The land away from the stables was wild, so glorious in its boldness. The trees were different, the shrubs were different. It was free and untamed. It possessed elements that Hennelie yearned for desperately in her life, she knew she was on the right path.

She had entered into the bushveld. It was the most exhilarating feeling. At last she was at one with nature and what's more she felt that she belonged here. It felt as if she had swallowed a jumping bean, she felt so alive and excited. The cacophony of bird sounds chirruping in the trees and flying home to roost was music to her ears.

Her earlier nervousness of the unknown seemed to be forgotten. Now she felt as if she was getting somewhere, as if she was getting closer to her dream, to her destination. She possessed an expectancy of great things to come; if only she could dance and jump and shout for joy.

Her inner voice cautioned her and warned her to go carefully and not to let her exuberance make her careless.

Conquering the bushveld would be no easy feat, and especially for a hamster. Hennelie would have to concentrate very hard if she was to successfully master this part of her journey.

The grass was very long and spikey which made the going tough. By the sun's position in the sky Hennelie knew that the day was very nearly coming to a close and before it did she needed to get some idea of the landscape in front of her.

Slowly she made her way to an old dilapidated watering hole where she clawed her way up to the top to view the north bound route ahead.

To her dismay and disappointment she saw a great big dam sprawled right across her intended pathway, "Oh no," she groaned. "What am I to do, how on earth will I get across the water?" She twitched in confusion.

Suddenly to her left Hennelie caught sight of a group of humans, screaming, jumping and laughing on the waters edge.

All held nets and pounced about madly shouting at the top of their voices. She watched as they grabbed at wriggly creatures, beating them and striking them before chucking them into buckets.

Hennelie rubbed her eyes in disbelief, all of a sudden she could feel one of her horrible panic attacks unfolding, her tiny body began to shake and quiver. Seeing all those humans killing those creatures had severely unnerved her. That and the stretch of water blocking her way sent her, as quick as lightning, down into the fearful dumps.

Hurriedly she scrambled down the bricks and dived into the long grass to lie low, think, and wait for the humans to disappear.

Whenever Hennelie got nervous she somehow developed the munchies. She began to nibble the grass, she nibbled on a sour weed, she nibbled the tip of an old stick, a mouldy dried leaf and a foul tasting pod.

Gradually the raucous voices died away until only the sound of rushing water could be heard, and the wind whistling through the tall trees, bringing the faint familiar smell of horses to Hennelie's sensitive nostrils.

Warm memories of her dear friends Monty and Mon Cherie were stirred up in Hennelie's mind and she lovingly visualised them warm and secure in their stable, with a delicious dinner to comfort them. For a fleeting moment she wished she hadn't left the stables.

The loud banging of a tin bucket brought Hennelie's daydreaming to a halt, "What was that?" she thought fearfully again, as she flattened herself against the prickly grass. A quick glance revealed Alfons the stable hand a short distance away pouring meal out of a bucket onto the grass. He banged the bucket several times and walked off.

It was then that Hennelie did a double take.

Out of the dam rose two enormous heads omitting booming, honking sounds as they heaved gigantic grey bodies to the surface of the rippling water. Out they came on short squat legs. They shuffled to the food on the ground put there by Alfons, and proceeded to scoop the food into the largest mouths that Hennelie had ever seen, with large gulping motions.

Hennelie very nearly suffered a seizure. She clutched her dainty pink paws to her breast and blinked and blinked at the sight before her eyes.

"Just how many different creatures are there in this world?" Hennelie asked herself in astonishment. All the creatures seemed to be getting larger and larger as her journey progressed. Despite the enormity of their size Hennelie surprisingly didn't feel afraid of them. Something inside egged her on to approach them.

She wove through the long grass until she was fairly close to them. Hennelie swallowed once before saying, "Excuse me?" and then again louder, "*Excuse me.*"

The two creatures stopped their gulping. Incredulous, large protruding pink rimmed eyes met Hennelie's tiny black ones.

"Oh what a cute tiny little thing," one gushed warmly, "Are you an insect?"

Hennelie wanted to reel over with mirth. Now *that* was a new one! An insect? She had never heard anything so funny.

"No," she giggled rubbing her little pink nose, "I'm not an insect. I'm Hennelie Hamster and I'm sorry to have interrupted your supper, it's just that I was so anxious to meet you both. I've never in my life seen such large creatures before. Do you mind me asking what you are?"

Now it was their turn to honk and shake with laughter, their short thick tails delightedly spinning like fans, "We're hippos," they grunted in happy unison. "Hippo short for Hippopotamus," said the larger of the two proudly.

"I am Danielle and this here is my partner Dan." The smaller one said flicking her small round pink ears.

"What a great pleasure it is to meet you both," said Hennelie.

"The pleasure is all ours my dear," Dan replied pleasantly.

Danielle invited Hennelie to join them for a bit of dinner which was mealie meal made from ground maize which Dan said was grown on the farm. "What luck," thought Hennelie, as she nibbled away alongside the two large creatures.

"My goodness it is tasty isn't it," said Hennelie in between mouthfuls.

She was so pleased with herself for having had the courage to approach the two creatures and the lovely meal was her reward.

Over dinner Hennelie recounted her story yet again of her great escape from the farm house, her experiences at the crossroad and, more importantly, she told them all about the wonderful creatures she had met along the way. When she explained she was expecting little ones, they congratulated her heartily.

Hennelie went on to tell the hippos despondently, "My plan was to head north for the hills way over there in the distance, but it seems I won't be able to with this huge stretch of water in my path."

"Oh my goodness, the water," there was laughter from the hippos, "that's no problem. We have the perfect solution. You can catch a ride with the two of us. After dinner we're off to the other side anyway," said Dan enthusiastically.

Hennelie was thrilled, "I hadn't thought of that, what a grand idea," she exclaimed happily. Suddenly her little face took on a serious expression, "but how will I climb aboard your back, I'm so small?" She rubbed her worried little face earnestly looking at Dan's great height.

"Never fear my dear," boomed Dan with a large grin. "I will lie down like this," he demonstrated heaving himself to the ground with a groan and a weighty sigh, "now you can climb up on to my face and wend your way over onto my back."

"What a brilliant idea," Hennelie cried out excitedly, "of course I'll be able to climb up now." She scurried forward clawing her way up past Dan's nostril and onto the bridge of his nose.

This of course was extremely ticklish for Dan. A dreadful sneeze began to build up. Hennelie's tiny scratchy little paws made Dan's face tingle all over. His bulbous eyes began to water, he held his breath and just when Hennelie had reached the top he let out a walloping sneeze. Had she not gripped with all her might onto Dan's ear she would have been propelled into space. Fortunately it was only one sneeze, another would have been fatal.

"Oh dear I'm sorry about that Hennelie, but your scurrying up my nose was very ticklish indeed," Dan said with a boisterous snort.

Hennelie balanced herself carefully on Dan's forehead.

"Are we all ready then?" asked Dan.

"Yes siree," replied Hennelie merrily.

This event proved to be exciting for all of them.

Up Dan got, heaving his massive bulk to the left and right with a huff and a sigh, "Come on Danielle, lets get back into the water and take Hennelie safely across to the other side. I'm sure nobody will see us, it's quite dark now."

Dan and Danielle shuffled back to the waters edge slowly and carefully. From Hennelie's lovely position on Dan's head she could see the bull rushes and water lilies that so prettily lined the dam.

"The frogs seem to be croaking louder than usual this evening," said Danielle softly as they sunk gently into the water, "I think they are very upset about the nasty incident that they witnessed this afternoon with the farm labourers and our friends the barbel."

They began to swim smoothly and elegantly through the glistening water.

"Oh yes," said Hennelie, "I saw something going on this afternoon; humans with nets, shouting and jumping near the waters edge, what was happening?"

Dan explained, "With all the rain we've had recently the dam got too full and overflowed. The water burst over the small wall and the humans were collecting all the fish and barbel that were swept along with it."

"Barbel?" asked Hennelie baffled, "what is a barbel?"

"A barbel is also called a catfish," said Danielle, "they have whiskers just like a cat."

A shiver went down Hennelie's spine. She didn't like cats. She asked, "What do humans catch them for?"

"They eat them," said Dan.

"Poor creatures," murmured Hennelie shocked, "how awful!"

They swam in silence for a while and then true to Dan's word the three of them reached the other side of the dam with no problem at all. Up onto the bank and through the mud they squelched. Hennelie shivered. Suddenly it seemed very dark and spooky. A small plantation of trees loomed up like a wall in front of them.

Dan being the sensitive creature that he was sensed Hennelie's anxiety and her fear of the unknown. He felt sorry for her she looked so vulnerable out here in the bush; so tiny and fragile.

"Hennelie don't be afraid," he said soothingly, "we wouldn't think of leaving you here all alone. We happen to have a good friend who lives in this plantation who we would like to introduce you to. She is very knowledgeable and she is very wise and I'm sure she will be delighted to assist you on part of your journey to the hills."

Dan gave a loud honk which was followed by a loud honk from Danielle.

Out from the trees swooped an elderly wise old owl. Hennelie cowered and flattened herself fearfully on Dan's forehead. The bird perched on a tree stump close by and alertly blinked her large round topaz eyes.

"Don't be frightened Hennelie dear," Danielle said kindly trying to sooth Hennelie's nerves, "you have nothing to fear from Olivia, she's a dear friend of ours who by the way has developed an allergy to all things furry, isn't that correct Olivia? She won't harm you."

Hennelie's little heart was pounding furiously.

"Olivia, please meet Hennelie, our little friend who is making her way to the far distant hills in the north," said Danielle.

"Not so far now," said Olivia.

"She'd be grateful for your protection and assistance for part of the way," said Dan.

"Ta whit, ta woo, how do you do?" sang Olivia in a friendly fashion. "Why I'd be honoured to accompany you part of the way Hennelie. I enjoy a little break from my usual routine every now and then."

Hennelie still felt slightly wary of Olivia, she mumbled a little "hello" although she did trust Dan and Danielle enough to know that they would never introduce her to a dangerous creature.

Dan, Danielle and Olivia chatted a while discussing the unusual rainy weather they were experiencing. "My goodness we've never had this much rain before at Christmas time," said Olivia, "although I mustn't complain, I get a lovely supply of flying ants, so I never go short of something scrummy to eat."

"I agree, the weather pattern seems to be quite different from previous years, quite alarming really," added Danielle.

"At least *we* have plenty of water in the dam," said Dan.

"Now Hennelie, we must head off back into the water dear, but rest assured you will be in good hands with Olivia. Do take care of yourself won't you? Good luck with the birth of your little ones and a very happy Christmas to you," said Danielle.

Dan heaved himself down onto the soggy ground to make it easy for Hennelie to disembark. She scurried down his nose onto the wet grass and thanked the two hippos for all their help.

"Goodbye my dear, it's been an absolute pleasure meeting you. You are a feisty courageous creature for one so small and you deserve all the very best in life," said Dan.

After goodbyes to Olivia, Dan and Danielle slid back into the water and away they swam after honking goodbye and good luck.

"Welcome to my home, the gum plantation," said Olivia warmly, "and please believe me when I say I won't eat you. It is quite true about my allergy. I get the most chronic indigestion from anything furry, so my diet consists of mainly flying ants these days."

Hennelie began to relax. Olivia looked so open and honest sitting on the stump, wide-eyed, serious and sincere. Hennelie's little heart slowed down from its heavy beating.

"My goodness what a lovely smell around these parts," said Hennelie sniffing appreciatively.

"Oh yes I'm glad you noticed," said Olivia, "that's precisely why I decided to make my home here. It's the smell of the eucalyptus trees more commonly called the gum tree. It gets much stronger further inside, follow me and see for yourself."

Olivia flitted and hopped from branch to branch leading Hennelie deeper into the plantation.

The smell was truly refreshing. Hennelie breathed in so many breaths she began to hyperventilate and feel giddy.

Encompassed in the dreamy, mystical depths of the plantation, Hennelie understood why Olivia chose to live there. It was so tranquil amongst the trees with their high gently swaying leafy tops. There was such a wonderful sense of peace. She felt her Creator close by her side.

"Hennelie do be careful not to get tangled up in one of the many spider webs down there, they're a real nuisance," Olivia warned from above. Fortunately the glistening spider webs were illuminated with dots of dew already which made them visible to Hennelie's sharp little eyes. She would make sure not to stumble into one.

Together they meandered through the plantation until they reached an open sandy path.

"The going will be a little easier for you now Hennelie," said Olivia thoughtfully.

The uncultivated rugged terrain together with the natural aromatic blend of wild plants and damp earth brought a wave of immense joy to tiny Hennelie.

The sandy grains massaged and caressed her delicate paws as she scampered down the path.

The barbed wire fence running along the side of the road, made it easy for Olivia to accompany her comfortably. At a relaxed moderate pace she fluttered from pole to pole.

There couldn't have been anyone better than Olivia to escort Hennelie. She turned out to be the most informative, intelligent creature that Hennelie had met so far. As they moved along she told Hennelie in great detail all about the flora and fauna of the region. Hennelie was astounded by the variety of textures, shapes, smells, and tastes. What a multitude of plants there were on either side of the narrow sandy path on which they were travelling.

Olivia pointed out a tree which was decorated with light fluffy yellow balls "That's an acacia tree. Mind you don't get stabbed by one of the many sharp pointed white thorns on its branches," she warned, "they can be quite lethal, though I do believe the leaves are rather tasty, going by what the heifers say. Now if its shade you're looking for then the most magnificent msasas to the left are ideal. Oh and what a pity the large tree in front of you is not in bloom. It's the jacaranda tree. Later on next year you can look forward to showing your little ones their magnificent spray of mauve flowers."

Olivia suddenly turned to Hennelie, "Oh forgive me my dear, I hope I'm not boring you stiff."

Hennelie assured Olivia she was not in the least bit bored. "Quite the contrary; I find it all so interesting and the knowledge will be beneficial to me. I will need to know everything about the bushveld if I'm going to make my home out here," added Hennelie, "please don't stop."

Olivia looked pleased; there was nothing she enjoyed more than to give a lecture on her favourite subject.

"Look at those flowers dear," she said to Hennelie. "Aren't they beautiful? They are called cosmos, and they grow wild out here." Hennelie gazed full of wonder at the pink, white and lilac blooms that were growing in abundance on either side of the path. It was quite remarkable.

Olivia went on pointing out edible common weeds. "If you ever happen to suffer from a stomach complaint, do remember the leaves of the black-jack, but do be careful not to get too close to the black spikes, they will attach themselves to you and you'll find them difficult to remove and that also goes for burrs."

"This here is wild basil; see it has a long stalk and blue flowers. Wild basil is excellent for discouraging irritating mosquitoes."

Olivia directed Hennelie's attention to some pretty yellow flowers with brownish red centres. "These are called stock-rose and not very pleasant to eat because of their bristly hair stems, I wouldn't touch them."

She went on to point out so many weeds and plants and trees that Hennelie was having difficulty keeping up, but at least it gave her an idea of what she could and couldn't eat in the bush and that was a very good start.

"This is called mexican clover and that's a bit of witch-weed. Over there is the thorn-apple, with its purple funnel shaped flowers and sharp spikey fruit. This is good for relieving asthma. Now please Hennelie do be very careful of this plant it is called apple of peru and it's highly toxic. The only thing it's good for is to kill and shoo away flies."

Olivia swooped down to the sandy path and hopped a few paces to another plant, "You may eat from this bush. It is called wild cape gooseberry, it's delicious I believe."

And on and on Olivia rambled without blinking or breathing, it seemed to Hennelie.

"The most palatable and nutritious of our indigenous grasses is this delicate guinea grass, along with the crow's foot over there. The pretty grass with the silver pink fluffy spikes is called red-top."

Hennelie laughed merrily, "Well I definitely won't starve out here."

Olivia turned to Hennelie worriedly and said, "Hennelie you must be very careful of what you eat in the bush. If insects haven't touched a plant then you must not. For example there are many varieties of mushrooms some of which are very highly poisonous. Don't touch mushrooms until you know which ones are safe."

Suddenly across the pathway ran a big black insect, Hennelie jumped.

"Oh don't worry about those," said Olivia scornfully, "it's only a matabele ant and they're everywhere during the day. They're not worth eating, they leave a bad taste in your mouth and they smell to high heaven when squashed. Now that brings to mind ticks; watch out for them. They are blood sucking parasites and they're everywhere at this time of year."

Hennelie shuddered with revulsion and began to feel itchy all over.

"And now Hennelie I must love and leave you, I need to have dinner and I'm meeting a cousin later who I can't introduce you to unfortunately because you, I'm sorry to say, would be one of her culinary delights."

Hennelie shuddered again and said quickly, "Oh no problem Olivia, please do go, I've kept you too long already. I am so appreciative of all the information. Thank you so much for your time and for passing on your knowledge. I appreciate it so much."

And with that Olivia spread her large wings and glided back to her mystical home in the plantation.

Hennelie scurried further along the sandy path. She really had a spring in her step now. With each minute she was getting closer to her dream. She could feel it in her tiny bones and it was so exciting. She felt renewed, energised. There was a lot of movement coming from the babies in her tummy; they were due all too soon. Hennelie just could not wait for them to arrive. "Please grant me patience," she prayed.

She looked around her and gave thanks. Suddenly there was so much to live for. How the tide had turned and she was so grateful.

Never in her wildest dreams did she think she'd feel this happy, with so much to look forward to. Hennelie was a different creature. She scurried on awhile looking, smelling, appreciating and even humming every now and then.

After a while Hennelie came to a large field which contained row upon row of extra large leafy plants, "My goodness, I wonder if these are edible. They look lovely and juicy," thought Hennelie feeling rather peckish. She decided to sample the green leaves.

Greedily she scurried across to a large drooping leaf and took a large bite. She chewed a couple of times and then spat out with such force, "Aaaaah! How horrible. Whatever is that plant?" Hennelie thought. Her mouth was burning. Her face contorted in disgust.

Loud barking laughter erupted unexpectedly to the left of her, intermingled with high pitched shrieks and splutters. A creature was killing itself with laughter at her expense.

"Who's there?" she shouted crossly.

She stood on her back legs and peered into the darkness with the dreadful bitter taste in her mouth lingering.

A black shape sauntered towards her. "Now what made you bite into the tobacco leaf you crazy little thing?" Drawled the creature lazily, chewing on something. "Do you want to kill yourself you pathetic little mite?" he added nastily. "Now what's made you want to commit suicide; got a complex about your size? Is that it? Ah come and tell daddy all about it," he droned sarcastically.

Hennelie sighed furiously, "Oh don't be silly, of course I don't want to commit suicide, I was simply feeling hungry and I thought I could eat that leaf."

By now the creature was right in front of her; he very crudely scratched his bottom, burped and continued to chew. His teeth looked mighty spooky; he had two large, stained yellow fangs which protruded threateningly from his large square mouth.

On one hand the creature looked very vicious, but on the other he seemed very lethargic and relaxed. Hennelie sensed he wasn't too interested in hurting her. On this occasion her size worked in her favour. She was far too small for him.

The burning continued in her mouth, she began to pant, "I'm sorry but I need water." In one of the furrows lay a puddle of water, she dashed up to it and sipped and sipped until gradually the burning sensation faded.

"Tell me are the leaves poisonous?" she asked the creature anxiously, concerned about the well being of the babies that she carried.

"Why yes! I believe they are," he retorted unpleasantly with an ugly lopsided leer, "but I'm sure you'll survive, you spat them out didn't you?" He shook his head and went on, "I've never understood the humans' dumb need to grow the stuff. Only they are stupid enough to pick the leaves, dry them out, roll them up and smoke them."

Hennelie listened flabbergasted, "What a queer lot, I agree," she said.

The creature gurgled on some of his spittle. It made Hennelie want to vomit. He sat down slumped in front of her, sloppily chewing and scratching his private parts. Hennelie couldn't stop herself from thinking what a coarse piece of work he was. He had a bad smell on top of everything else.

Eventually she picked up the courage to ask who he was.

He burped before replying, "I'm Diro. Diro means baboon in Shona; my pastime is to irritate and tease the farm labourers by breaking the leaves and stalks of their beloved tobacco. I'd ask you to join me but you're too incy wincy, poor little thing."

Hennelie wished he'd stop talking to her like that.

"It amuses me no end, watching them set up a howl and a chase, knowing full well they could never catch me. I'm too quick for them," he said grinning boastfully.

Diro didn't bother to ask Hennelie who she was and she was relieved, preferring to get as far away as possible from the offensive, loathsome creature. She remembered the saying, "You are judged by the company you keep."

Hastily she said, "Well nice to have met you Diro, I must get along now." She was about to scurry off when he said with a sneer, "Well you're a very brave rodent to be squirrelling your way about the bush at this time of day."

Rodent, how dare he. How it irritated Hennelie to be called a rodent.

She decided wisely not to correct him or to show that it infuriated her. She knew it was just better to walk away.

"Don't you think you're a bit of an ignoramus? Not very clever are you? Firstly you're unaware that you're on a tobacco farm, and now I bet you don't know a thing about all the treacherous snakes that dominate the area," he leered maliciously.

"Snakes? What snakes?" asked Hennelie abruptly.

He laughed raucously, scratching himself all over gleefully, "well do be careful of the green boom slang, they enjoy feeding off creatures such as yourself, as do the deadly Egyptian cobras and puff adders." He gurgled maliciously.

He licked his lips and continued, "all move rapidly and have split second strikes. Out of them all I think the puff adder is the most attractive to look at; it would love the likes of you." He roared with laughter again.

Hennelie's flesh crawled. She was beginning to feel very scared again. A moment or so ago she had been so happy; why did this monster have to pop up in her pathway, to throw her off balance? Why do some creatures derive so much pleasure from causing unhappiness and fear? It was terrible, she wished he'd stop.

But he didn't, he went on unkindly, "and then of course there's the nasty old python that very slowly squeezes all the breath out of you before crushing your bones and swallowing you whole!" He spluttered and gurgled with pleasure at the look of fear on Hennelie's face.

Her whiskers twitched uncontrollably and she knew she had to get away from him as quickly as possible. She scurried away as fast as her little legs could take her.

Echoing behind her she heard the sound of his large booming evil laughter ricocheting in the darkness.

As she ran tears ran down her face. "Please dear Creator, help me. Make me strong again. Please protect me from all nasty creatures. Oh please help me, surround me with good kind creatures."

In the middle of her prayers she heard a voice call out to her, "Little creature, little creature." Hennelie stopped running, and looked about her. The voice buzzed, "Little creature, over here." Hennelie stood on her little back legs, and there on a blade of grass sat a podgy red and black ladybird.

"Calm down," she said kindly to Hennelie, "I happened to hear every bit of what that insensitive, nasty Diro said to you," she buzzed soothingly. "Don't let creatures like that steal your joy. You only play into their hands when they see you upset. Don't give them the pleasure. You just have to feel sorry for them, they are unhappy empty vessels."

The voice buzzed on, "You're looking very upset and anxious, and when one is like that, one cannot think clearly. Now I suggest we find you somewhere to rest so that you can gather your wits about you again. I know of a perfect place, follow me."

Hennelie was so grateful to this creature that arrived in her life just at the right time. She followed the ladybird who buzzed in small spurts from blade of grass to blade of grass.

Finally she said, "Here is a nice safe old msasa tree that will gladly offer you refuge for the night. There's a nice little hollow over here where I'm sure you'll be lovely and comfortable. I'll keep guard outside so please relax and have a good rest. You look bone weary, now off to sleep you go and don't worry about another thing, life's too short."

Hennelie felt so grateful to this compassionate fellow creature. Her heart swelled with love. Before Hennelie disappeared into the little hollow at the base of the tree she thanked the ladybird and asked shyly what her name was after introducing herself.

"Lucinda is my name," buzzed the little ladybird merrily before she settled down herself to rest lightly on a spiky yellow flower. "Off to sleep Hennelie, and we'll chat again tomorrow, goodnight and sleep tight," she added sweetly.

Lucinda had completely charmed Hennelie. Not only was she kind, but she was also very beautiful. She was looking forward to getting to know her better in the morning. Hennelie curled up tightly into a little ball and fell into a deep sleep in the cosy little hollow.

She awoke with a start late the following morning to a commotion carrying on in the branches of the msasa tree above her. Her eyes flew open. For a moment she didn't know where she was. Suddenly she remembered the nasty episode of the meeting the night before with Diro the horrible baboon, and then of course the lovely meeting with Lucinda the ladybird. It was much better to think on the nicer things in life, Hennelie decided.

She scurried to the opening of the hollow to peep out. Lucinda spotted her from the same spikey yellow flower that she had settled on the night before.

"Oh dear, I'm sorry that they disturbed you Hennelie. What a bother those starlings can be at times. They must be the most raucous birds in the world," Lucinda buzzed disapprovingly.

After greeting Lucinda with a little yawn, and a cheery "good morning" Hennelie glanced up into the high branches of the msasa tree and sure enough, twenty odd starlings bickered crudely amongst one another.

Hennelie caught Lucinda's eye and both giggled merrily.

"Just as well they woke me up," Hennelie said smiling, "I'd probably have gone on sleeping all day. What time is it?" she asked.

"Looking at the position of the sun directly above us it must be around midday," replied Lucinda. "Isn't it wonderful to have the sun's rays on our backs for a change after all the rain we've been having?"

Lucinda and Hennelie remained where they were for a while, basking in the sun and giving themselves a chance to get to know each other. During this time Hennelie mentioned with pride that she was expecting babies in the next day or two.

"Oh how wonderful for you," buzzed Lucinda with delight. "Congratulations, now I understand why you're so anxious to find a suitable home so quickly. Do you know Hennelie, I think I can help you," she said with a gleam in her eye. "I know a short cut to the hills, I know the area well."

Hennelie was thrilled by Lucinda's suggestion. Boy did she need a good girlfriend out here. What a blessing.

The two friends set off towards the hills. Lucinda took the lead, warning Hennelie about all the extremely dangerous old deep ant holes that lay camouflaged in the long grass.

It was a rough path for Hennelie to travel at this stage in her pregnancy. Her large rounded tummy almost dragged on the stony ground. They dodged old ant holes, snake holes, devil thorns and red termites, which Lucinda said nipped like mad.

"Don't get too close to that bush," warned Lucinda, "It's a prickly pear plant, and it's very difficult to remove the almost invisible little prickles, and they sting. It's a pity because the fruit is so delicious to eat."

On they travelled slowly and carefully. What struck Hennelie the most were all the butterflies bearing dazzling designs and colours, they fluttered freely by with not a care in the world.

When they stopped to take a breath a dragonfly flew across their path and settled on the most glorious flower that Hennelie had ever seen.

"It's beautiful, isn't it," said Lucinda, "It's called the flame lily. They grow wild in the bush and are in abundance at Christmas time."

Harmony abounded all about thought Hennelie. The warm wind rustled through the long grass, in tune with the harmonious choir of continuous humming, which Lucinda said was from the well hidden christmas beetles. "They never stop singing at this time of year."

"I don't blame them. I love Christmas time too. Oh Lucinda let's make sure we are comfortably settled in the hills by tonight, its Christmas eve," said Hennelie earnestly. She clutched her two little paws together at her breast.

"I'm sure we'll make it if we keep going without stopping. Can you manage that Hennelie?" Lucinda asked with concern. Looking at Hennelie's tummy she was worried the babies would arrive any minute.

As they continued on the rugged journey, Lucinda watched anxiously as Hennelie manoeuvred her big belly over sharp sticks and stones. "Please babies, hold on awhile," she prayed.

"Hello ladies," a voice penetrated through Lucinda's thoughts. "You both look as if you're in a bit of a rush."

"Oh hello Desmond," replied Lucinda, "how nice to bump into you; busy as usual I see."

Hennelie couldn't see anybody. She stopped, stood on her back legs, rubbed her face and twitched her whiskers.

"Over here Hennelie," buzzed Lucinda, "come over here and meet a friend of mine, Desmond Dung Beetle."

Scurrying over Hennelie came face to face with a large black beetle. He was busy rolling a big smelly ball of manure.

"Pleased to meet you Desmond," said Hennelie politely, wondering how Desmond could touch the highly stinky stuff. Hennelie rubbed her little nose frantically.

Watching her Lucinda wanted to burst into gales of laughter. She had to buzz about a bit to keep herself from giggling out loud. That's when she caught sight of Gladys and Gilmore Guinea Fowl and their two children Gavin and Gertrude.

"My goodness, how lovely to see you all," Lucinda buzzed happily. "Hennelie come over and meet the Guinea Fowl family," she called out pleasantly.

"Ah, and look who else is here. Camilla Chameleon, who we haven't seen in absolute ages," said Gilmore.

"Camilla, how are you?" buzzed Lucinda delightedly. "My word, what a lovely surprise to see you all."

Hennelie gazed at the creatures in front of her with astonishment; how well turned out they all were. The Guinea Fowl family all wore smart helmets of red and blue upon their heads and Camilla the Chameleon, the strange stand offish creature, possessed large rotating eyes and a very eccentric looped up tail.

Lucinda buzzed proudly, "Won't you all please meet my new friend and a new-comer to our community, Hennelie Hamster, who has travelled a very, very long way to live with us in the bushveld."

They all welcomed Hennelie warmly. "Oh my," exclaimed Hennelie, "I'm just so amazed at the wonderful variety of creatures there are. What a blessing it is to meet you all."

"And you haven't seen half of them yet!" chirr chirred Gladys Guinea Fowl merrily.

Lucinda apologised to her friends for not being able to stay and chat for a little longer, explaining that they were anxious to get Hennelie safely settled in a nice new home by tonight Christmas eve.

"Perhaps we can get together tomorrow on Christmas day," she said hopefully, "and celebrate in our usual merry way beneath the marula tree." She added with a mischievous wink.

"Definitely, most definitely, we'll all be there," they chorused.

From where they stood they could see the large grey rocks that were splashed artistically with orange, cream and green specks. "What adorable wall paper," Hennelie thought.

In her heart she knew she was on the verge of a breakthrough, she knew she had nearly reached her destination. "Lucinda," she cried out, "I can feel it, we're almost there."

Lucinda was becoming anxious. "Please Hennelie, for goodness sake do keep calm." She didn't want the babies to arrive just yet. "Evening is settling in and we must keep our wits about us."

They travelled a while in silence. The rough, rocky terrain required their full attention now.

For the first time ever Hennelie witnessed the splendour of an African sunset. It melted across the horizon replacing the blue of the late afternoon sky; magnificent blends of gold, orange, yellow and red spread across and behind the purple grey mountains in the distance.

Hennelie was speechless and humbled as she gazed in wonderment at the divine picture unfolding in the west.

"Come along Hennelie," she heard Lucinda buzz, "we must keep moving."

Hennelie clambered heavily and breathlessly upwards. Between fallen chipped off rocks; avoiding prickly aloes and cactus plants, over bits of peeled bark that had fallen off trees. Upwards and onwards she trudged over stones, dry leaves and branches, between ferns and wild creepers that garnished the rocky path.

On her right grew an unusual tree laden with yellow fruit, a lot of which had fallen to the ground and lay ripe for the picking. "That's the marula tree that I mentioned earlier," said Lucinda with a smile. "This is where we gather mostly for our celebrations. A nibble on the sweet fruit can make one very merry indeed," Lucinda said naughtily.

A little further up the hill they climbed until at last they had arrived at the ideal spot.

Lucinda buzzed softly, "Could you call this little place home Hennelie?"

Tears of joy sprung into Hennelie's eyes as she looked at the small overhanging rock that lay protectively over a miniature cave. It was nestled among patches of mossy ground. A beautiful creeper, which bore pretty dainty white flowers, surrounded the area providing security and shelter.

"Oh Lucinda," she wept, "This is the exact home that I have been dreaming about for a very long while. It's perfect. Oh, thank you Lucinda, thank you," she cried joyfully as a crescendo of frog croaks and christmas beetle song filled the air.

Hennelie bowed her head and with her tiny paws clutched at her breast she prayed and whispered softly "thank you."

That very night on Christmas eve, Hennelie gave birth to seven baby hamsters in her snug new home. The following morning, on CHRISTMAS DAY, Hennelie, Lucinda and the rest of the community gathered beneath the marula tree to celebrate and give thanks.

Hennelie had at last reached her promised land.

Made in the USA
Charleston, SC
22 October 2012